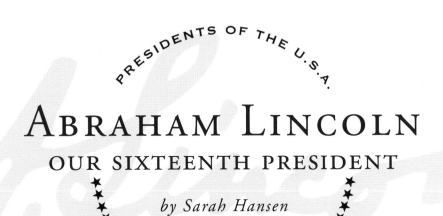

PRESIDENTS OF THE U.S.A.

ABRAHAM LINCOLN
OUR SIXTEENTH PRESIDENT

by Sarah Hansen

THE CHILD'S WORLD ®

The Child's World

PUBLISHED IN THE UNITED STATES OF AMERICA

THE CHILD'S WORLD®
1980 Lookout Drive • Mankato, MN 56003-1705
800-599-READ • www.childsworld.com

ACKNOWLEDGMENTS
The Child's World®: Mary Berendes, Publishing Director

The Creative Spark: Mary McGavic, Project Director and Page Production;
Shari Joffe, Editorial Director; Deborah Goodsite, Photo Research

The Design Lab: Kathleen Petelinsek, Design

Content Adviser: James Cornelius, Curator, Abraham Lincoln Presidential Library
and Museum, Springfield, Illinois

PHOTOS
Cover and page 3: Huntington Library/SuperStock

Interior: Abraham Lincoln Presidential Library & Museum: 13; The Art
Archive: 17, 28 (Culver Pictures); The Bridgeman Art Library: 14, 35 (Chicago
History Museum), 19, 20 bottom (Peter Newark American Pictures); Corbis:
37 (Bettmann); Getty Images: 7, 9 and 38, 22; The Granger Collection, New
York: 10, 16, 18, 20 top, 23, 36; The Image Works: 4 (H. Armstrong Roberts), 5
(Andre Jenny), 25 and 38 (Topham), 32 (The Print Collector/Heritage-Images);
iStockphoto: 44 (Tim Fan); Library of Congress: 15, 26, 30 and 39, 31, 34;
North Wind Picture Archives: 11 (North Wind); U.S. Air Force photo: 45.

LIBRARY OF CONGRESS CATALOGING-IN-PUBLICATION DATA
Hansen, Sarah.
  Abraham Lincoln / by Sarah Hansen.
      p. cm. — (Presidents of the U.S.A.)
  Includes bibliographical references and index.
  ISBN 978-1-60253-045-4 (library bound : alk. paper)
  1. Lincoln, Abraham, 1809–1865—Juvenile literature. 2. Presidents—United
States—Biography—Juvenile literature. I. Title. II. Series.

  E457.905.H285 2008
  973.7092—dc22
  [B]

                              2008001164

*Many people rank
Abraham Lincoln as the
greatest U.S. president.*

TABLE OF CONTENTS

CHAPTER ONE

A FRONTIER CHILDHOOD

The boy who would one day lead the nation through one of its most difficult times spent his childhood on the **frontier** of the United States. Abraham Lincoln was born to Thomas and Nancy Hanks Lincoln on February 12, 1809, near Hodgenville, Kentucky. His home was a rough cabin with a dirt floor. A couple of years later, the Lincoln family moved to a farm along Knob Creek in Kentucky.

In those days, pioneer families had to build their own houses, grow most of their food, and make any clothes, tools, and furniture that they needed. Every member of the family helped with all the work there was to do. When Abraham was a young child, his chores were to carry water and to collect firewood for his mother. Sometimes he helped his father plant seeds for crops.

Abraham Lincoln rose from humble beginnings to become one of the greatest figures in American history.

Abraham Lincoln's boyhood home is located at the Lincoln Boyhood National Memorial, near Little Pigeon Creek, Indiana.

Lincoln hated the nickname "Abe." People who knew him well never called him by that name.

When Abraham was seven years old, the family decided to go north to Indiana, which was about to become a state. They packed all their belongings on two horses, crossed the Ohio River on a **ferry,** and traveled nearly 100 miles (161 km) through the wilderness to the land where they would build a new home. The forest was so dense that they had to use a wagon with runners on it, like a sleigh, to cross the thick underbrush. While building their cabin, they lived in a three-sided shelter made of logs. It was wintertime, so they kept a fire burning at the open end of the shelter to provide warmth and to keep wild animals away. When spring arrived, Abraham helped clear the land for growing crops.

When Lincoln was a child, young boys on the frontier wore only long, homespun shirts that came down below their knees. Their first pair of pants, often worn when they were seven or eight years old, was usually made of buckskin.

Although men and boys on the frontier hunted as a way of life, Lincoln hated it. He was so upset after shooting a turkey one day, he never shot at a living thing again.

About two years later, Abraham's mother died. His sister, who was just 11 years old, tried to take over the cooking, cleaning, mending, and washing. But she was too young to handle the work alone. Their father went back to Kentucky for a short time, hoping to find a new wife. There he married a **widow** named Sarah Bush Johnston and returned to Indiana with her and her three young children. Sarah set to work at once, cleaning up the run-down cabin and ragged children.

Sarah Lincoln had an enormous influence on Abraham. Along with a wagonload of good furniture, she brought a few books and encouraged him to read them. He eagerly read and reread every one. Even though she was not educated herself, Sarah could see that Abraham was an extraordinary boy who was hungry to learn. She sent the children off to a school that was miles away. When one school closed, she tried to find another. Most frontier people were too busy with the hard work of surviving to make time for education, but Abraham's stepmother knew that Abraham was special. She helped him learn as much as he could. Abraham later said that she had been "his best friend in the world" and that no son could love a mother more than he loved her.

In many ways Abraham's early years were typical of a boyhood on the frontier. He had to cut trees to clear the land, build fences, and plant and plow the fields. But he was not a typical frontier boy. He was known for his kindness to animals and was unusually sensitive. He did not like to hunt or fish, and could not stand

Abraham often studied by firelight after working on his family's farm all day. Although he couldn't often attend school, he worked hard to learn as much as he could.

the sight of blood. As he grew older, he did not drink, swear, or use tobacco as other young men did.

Perhaps the most unusual thing about Abraham was his burning desire to learn and improve himself. One of his cousins later remembered that from the time Abraham was 12 years old, he almost always had a book in his hand or his pocket. When he was plowing a field, he read while the horse rested at the end of a row. At lunch, Abraham read while he ate. When he wasn't working, he might walk as far as 20 miles (32 km) to borrow a book!

Abraham also read every newspaper he could get his hands on, and in this way became interested in **politics.** As a teenager he liked to listen to the townspeople argue about public affairs in the local store. He attended political meetings and heard discussions

The disease that killed Lincoln's mother and many other settlers around Pigeon Creek was called "milk sick." It was caused by drinking the milk of cows that had eaten a poisonous plant called snakeroot.

When Thomas Lincoln was eight years old, he saw his father killed by Native Americans. Thomas had to make his own way in the world from an early age, finding work wherever he could. He never had the opportunity to go to school. This may have been the reason why Thomas was never able to understand his son's love of reading.

on issues and elections. Abraham took advantage of every opportunity to expand his experience and to use his mind.

By the time he was 16, Abraham was six feet (183 cm) tall, a good wrestler, and a fast runner. He was strong and lean, and his father often hired him out to work on nearby farms. Abraham enjoyed walking around the countryside, his axe on his shoulder. He often stopped to talk and joke with people, who gathered around to hear one of his stories. He became known as a funny and entertaining storyteller. Sometimes he would stand on a tree trunk and give speeches, imitating the **politicians** who visited the area.

When he was 17, Abraham got a job working on a ferry on the Ohio River, earning about 37 cents a day. It was difficult work, but it gave him the opportunity to see the interesting people and the new steamships that traveled up and down the river. One day after he rowed two travelers out to catch a steamboat in the middle of the river, each of them threw a 50-cent piece into his boat. He couldn't believe that he, a poor farm boy, had earned a dollar in less than a day. Years later, telling this story in the White House, he said, "it was the most important incident of my life . . . the world seemed wider and fairer before me."

Abraham returned home more determined than ever to be more than a poor pioneer like his father. The new sights and opportunities he had seen on the river fueled his ambition. In two years he would have another opportunity to see the wider world.

A businessman hired Abraham and another young man to take a flatboat loaded with cargo 1,200 miles (1,931 km) down the Ohio and Mississippi rivers to New Orleans. On the way, Abraham noticed the changing countryside. The weather was warmer and the farms were different than those in Indiana. Black slaves worked in the fields growing cotton, sugar, and tobacco.

When at last they reached New Orleans, Abraham was awed by the sight of such a big city. At that time, New Orleans was the fifth-largest city in the United

As a boy, Lincoln developed the habit of reading slowly and carefully, thinking about each point before moving on. Then he would repeat it over and over again to make sure he really understood it. Throughout his life he used this method to learn new things.

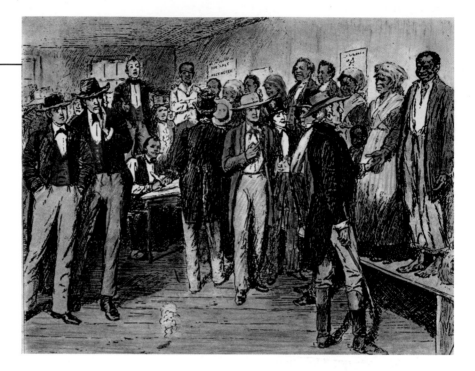

This illustration shows a slave auction much like one Abraham Lincoln might have seen during his first visit to New Orleans.

States, with 30,000 people. For a boy who had never seen a town of more than 150 people, this was enormous. There were more than 1,000 flatboats from the North, and giant sailing ships that would take goods from the United States to other parts of the world. He may have seen a slave auction where black people were sold like cattle. It was Abraham's first look at the world beyond his own community.

After spending a few days in the city, Abraham went back up the river in a steamboat. He gave the 25 dollars he had earned to his father. Abraham helped his family move once more, this time to Illinois. After helping them get settled and spending a hard, cold winter in their new home, he was ready to set out on his own.

EDUCATION ON THE FRONTIER

Abraham Lincoln once said his education was "by littles," meaning he went to school a little bit at a time. When Lincoln was a boy, Kentucky had no public education. Parents paid teachers with food, clothing, or money. Teachers often did not stay in one school for long.

The first school Abraham went to was called a "blab school." It was a log cabin with one log left out of a wall to let the light in. The students had to say their lessons out loud, or "blab," so that the teacher knew they were working. The teacher stood in front, ready to punish anyone who was not "blabbing."

In those days, most schools didn't have many books, and there was very little paper. Students would do their schoolwork on whatever they could find. Lincoln was said to have written his math problems on a board or the back of a shovel with a piece of burned wood from the fireplace. Then he scraped them off with a knife when he was finished so he could do the next problem. Children often made their own arithmetic books. Some of the pages of Lincoln's book still exist today, including the one shown here.

CHAPTER TWO

LAW AND POLITICS

Abraham Lincoln was 22 years old when he walked into New Salem, Illinois, carrying everything he owned under one arm. With a population of about 100 people, New Salem was bigger than anywhere Lincoln had ever lived. At first, people didn't know what to think of this lanky young man with messy hair and ill-fitting clothes. He had an odd, high-pitched voice and bad grammar. One man, who later became his friend, said Lincoln was "as rough a specimen of humanity as could be found" when he first came to town. Another person reported that Lincoln's yellow linen pants were usually rolled up one leg and down the other. But it wouldn't take long for the citizens of New Salem to find out that Abraham Lincoln was more than the coarse country boy that he appeared to be.

Lincoln got a job as a clerk in a general store, where he earned 15 dollars a month and slept in the back room. He was friendly and funny, and soon people were coming to the store to hear him tell his jokes and stories. He quickly became part of the community. When people needed help building houses or harvesting crops, he was a willing helper. He also gained a reputation as a

fair and honest man. Residents often asked him to be the judge of races and other contests.

As always, Lincoln wanted to improve himself. He was embarrassed by his lack of education and one of the first things he did was to study grammar. With the help of a borrowed book he taught himself to speak and write better English. He joined the local **debating** society to exchange ideas and practice public speaking.

In 1832, Lincoln decided to run for the **state legislature.** He talked to his neighbors and made speeches, trying out his newly improved speaking skills. Lincoln didn't win, but most of the people in his **precinct** voted for him.

Lincoln went back to storekeeping, this time as a part owner of a general store. The store failed and left

After he lost the election for the Illinois state legislature in 1832, Lincoln became part owner of this general store in New Salem.

To pay back the debt from his failed store, Lincoln had to work very hard. He split logs to make rail fences, worked on farms, and even became postmaster of New Salem. Lincoln's hard work earned the respect of the townspeople.

Shortly after Lincoln moved to New Salem, a gang of men calling themselves the Clary's Grove Boys challenged him to a wrestling match with their leader, Jack Armstrong. Lincoln fought so well that he earned the friendship and admiration of the whole gang. Armstrong remained Lincoln's friend and supporter for many years.

Lincoln with a huge debt of $1,100. He promised to pay it all back to the bank. He split fence rails and worked on farms. He also became the New Salem postmaster, where he enjoyed reading the newspapers that came in the mail. It would take him 15 years to repay the debt, but he would earn a reputation for honesty.

In 1834, at age 25, Lincoln again ran for the state legislature. This time he won. He bought his first suit and traveled to the state capital in a stagecoach. Then he won three more two-year **terms.** Lincoln was a good debater, and he did well in the legislature. It was there that he made his first public statement on slavery, saying that it was unjust and a problem for the country.

Legislators made three dollars a day, and only during the months when the legislature was in **session.** Lincoln had to find an additional job. He thought of becoming a lawyer but worried about his lack of education. Finally, he decided to try. At the time, people could study law by themselves or with the help of a lawyer. They were not required to go to college. Lincoln borrowed law books and studied them on his own for nearly three years. When he passed his law exam, he moved to Springfield, Illinois, on a borrowed

Abraham Lincoln studied hard to be a lawyer. At the time, many lawyers were self-taught because few people could afford to go to college. It took three years of study, but Lincoln finally became a lawyer.

Lincoln eventually became a very successful trial lawyer. This illustration shows him defending a client during a murder trial.

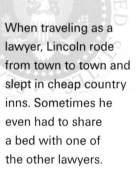

When traveling as a lawyer, Lincoln rode from town to town and slept in cheap country inns. Sometimes he even had to share a bed with one of the other lawyers.

horse with just seven dollars in his pocket. There he was hired to work under an experienced lawyer.

Lincoln took all kinds of **cases,** from small disputes to big trials in the Illinois **Supreme Court.** For four to six months of the year, he traveled with a judge and other lawyers to try cases in small towns. As always, Lincoln enjoyed the chance to meet and talk to people. He became well known throughout Illinois.

After Lincoln moved to Springfield, he met a lively young woman named Mary Todd, the daughter of a banker. Lincoln and Mary were married in 1842. Soon they bought a house where they would live for the next 17 years. Their first son, Robert, was just a baby when they moved there.

Over the years, three more sons—Edward, William, and Thomas ("Tad"), were born in that house. The family lived comfortably and usually had a servant to help with the housework. But Lincoln often cared for his own horse , chopped all the firewood, and milked the family cow.

At the end of four terms in the legislature, Lincoln wanted to become a United States congressman. He was elected to the U.S. House of Representatives in 1846, but served only for one term. At that time, one of the major issues was the war with Mexico. The United States had gone to war with Mexico in 1846, and as a result had conquered much of its land, including the present states of California, Nevada, Utah, most of Arizona and New Mexico, and parts of Wyoming and Colorado.

Lincoln spoke out against the supposed cause of this war, calling it immoral and unnecessary. He supported

Mary Lincoln wanted her husband to look and act more like a professional man. She tried to lengthen his pants and help him wear matching clothes. She also tried to improve his table manners, which were crude according to the standards of high society.

This is the first known photograph of Abraham Lincoln. It was taken in 1846, when he was 37 years old.

Lincoln and Mary Todd (above) had a lot in common. They were both interested in politics, loved poetry and writing, and hated slavery. Both were eager to achieve success in life, too.

a bill that would prohibit slavery in any of the new lands taken from Mexico, but it did not pass. He had also proposed a bill of his own that would ban slavery in the District of Columbia, but dropped it when members of both the Democrats and the Whigs, his own party, criticized it.

When he wasn't reelected, Lincoln went home to Springfield. His term in Congress had been a disappointment. Lincoln's opposition to the war had been unpopular in Illinois, and his political career seemed to be over. Lincoln went back to being a lawyer. He worked hard in his law office and became very rich and successful.

Five years later, Lincoln got involved in politics again. The nation was involved in a serious debate about whether to allow slavery in any new states that joined the **Union.** In 1820, a law called the Missouri Compromise had made it illegal to have slaves in any state north of a specific **latitude.** The people who supported this law hoped that if slavery could be limited, it would eventually end. But then a law said that all new **territories** should decide for themselves if they wanted slavery. It was called the Kansas-Nebraska Act of 1854. Lincoln believed that slavery should not be allowed to spread. In 1856, he joined a **political party,** the anti-slavery **Republican Party.**

In 1858, Lincoln ran for the United States Senate against Stephen A. Douglas. He challenged Douglas to a series of debates, known as the Lincoln-Douglas debates. Reporters from as far away as New York and Boston wrote about these events for their newspapers. Lincoln lost the election, but the **campaign** made him famous around the country.

When the Republican National **Convention** met in 1860, the members of the party **nominated** Abraham Lincoln to run for president. Unlike today, presidential candidates at that time felt that it was undignified to campaign for themselves. Lincoln stayed quietly at home in Springfield while his supporters worked for him. Lincoln won the election, with nearly all of his votes coming from the Northern states.

The law office that Lincoln shared with his partner was messy and disorganized. Papers, journals, books, letters, and legal **documents** were spread all over the place. Lincoln sometimes kept important papers in the lining of his hat so that he would know where to find them.

When Lincoln was running for president, a young girl wrote to him saying that he would look better in "whiskers" because his face was so thin. He took her advice and always wore a beard after that.

The Lincoln-Douglas debates made Abraham Lincoln a national figure.

THE LINCOLN-DOUGLAS DEBATES

When Lincoln heard that Senator Stephen Douglas of Illinois had proposed the Kansas-Nebraska bill in the U.S. Senate, he was worried that the Southern slave states were gaining too much power in the country. The South's money came mostly from **plantations**, which depended on slaves to grow and harvest the crops. Lincoln worried that if slavery were allowed to spread, it might one day exist in all the states, old and new, North and South.

Lincoln decided to run for the Senate against Stephen Douglas. He challenged Douglas to a series of debates to be held in seven Illinois towns. There was great excitement in each town, as thousands of people came from miles around to hear the two men speak. Bands played, cannons fired, and the towns were decorated with colorful banners and flags. Newspaper reporters followed the debates, sending stories and copies of the candidates' speeches to newspapers in eastern cities such as Boston and New York.

The candidates could hardly have been more different. Douglas was a short man, just five feet, four inches (163 cm) tall. Lincoln was a full foot taller. The reporters called them "The Little Giant" and "Long Abe." Douglas wore expensive clothing and fine, ruffled shirts, while Lincoln wore a plain suit that was often wrinkled. Douglas argued that the nation could survive, half slave and half free, if each state had the right to decide for itself about slavery. Lincoln said that slavery was wrong, an evil to the whole country.

Lincoln lost the election, but it made him famous all over the nation. He was back in politics, and he was a more powerful speaker than ever because he cared deeply about the issue of slavery.

CHAPTER THREE

THE CIVIL WAR

Lincoln knew he had a hard job ahead of him. Saying goodbye to the people of Springfield, he said, "I now leave, not knowing when, or whether ever, I may return." The train trip to Washington took almost two weeks, stopping in many small towns along the way to greet the crowds that came out to see him. When Lincoln reached Baltimore, Maryland, detectives told Lincoln that a group of people was planning to kill him because of his opposition to slavery. He decided not to take any chances. He quickly crossed the city in a covered coach. Then, he took a different train than he had planned to, secretly traveling through the night accompanied by armed guards.

Instead of triumphant entrance into the capital, the president-elect arrived unannounced just after dawn, wearing a heavy coat, a scarf, and a soft hat pulled low on his face. He was embarrassed that he had to sneak into the city. His critics made fun of him in the newspapers for arriving in disguise. His awkwardness and country manners didn't help his image in the capital.

But Lincoln had more important things to worry about. Months earlier, after Lincoln won the election,

Lincoln's inauguration took place in front of the Capitol. At the time, builders were still constructing the majestic new dome that would soon become a symbol of national pride.

South Carolina had immediately **seceded** from the Union, and five more Southern states had followed. They declared they were no longer part of the United States and wrote their own **constitution.** They established a new country called the **Confederate** States of America and elected Jefferson Davis as their president.

It was under these serious circumstances that Lincoln arrived in Washington to take office in March of 1861. In his **inaugural address,** he urged the Southern states not to start a war, saying they had no right "to destroy the government, while I shall have the most solemn one to **preserve,** protect, and defend it."

A month later, his words were tested. Confederate troops had surrounded Fort Sumter in the harbor of Charleston, South Carolina. They refused to allow Union ships to get through with **provisions.** When Lincoln sent a supply ship to the soldiers at Fort Sumter, Confederate troops opened fire on the fort. The American Civil War had begun.

President Lincoln responded quickly. He declared war and asked for 75,000 volunteers to join the army. Some people believed that the United States Constitution gave these powers to Congress, not to the president. But Lincoln believed that his Constitutional duty "to hold, occupy, and possess what belongs to the federal government" gave him the responsibility to preserve the Union. For him, the most important reason for fighting

Fort Sumter was off the coast of Charleston, South Carolina. In 1861, it was running short of supplies. The U.S. government needed to restock its supplies or shut it down. President Lincoln thought the South would consider it a sign of weakness if he closed the fort, so he sent supplies and soldiers. The Confederates saw this as an act of war. They attacked the fort on April 12, 1861, and the Civil War began.

Legend has it that at his inauguration, Lincoln looked around for a place to put his hat before he started to speak. His old opponent, Stephen Douglas, stepped up and held it for him while he delivered his inaugural address.

At the Battle of Bull Run, there was no system for moving the wounded back to Washington. Some wounded men walked 27 miles (43 km) back, while others were left to die. The situation improved as the war progressed. An ambulance service was organized and men were carried on stretchers to ambulances (horse-drawn carts), and taken to field hospitals.

the war was to prove that a democracy like the United States could work. A democracy is a country in which the people of the country decide who their leaders will be through free elections. Lincoln wanted to prove that the Union wouldn't fall apart when there were serious disagreements among its people.

Most Northerners thought that the war would be over quickly. The North had more than twice as many people as the South. It also had factories to produce weapons and railroads to transport troops. But the South had the country's best generals. Most battles took place in the South, so they also had the advantage of fighting in their own territory, on land they knew well.

The first battle took place on July 21 at Bull Run, about 25 miles (40 km) southwest of Washington, D.C. People drove to the battlefield in carriages. Some even took picnic lunches to eat while they watched the battle! After a few hours of fighting, the Union troops fled back to Washington. People now realized that the war was much more serious than a day's entertainment, and was likely to last years instead of months.

Disturbed by this defeat, Lincoln realized he needed to learn more about fighting a war. He checked out several books from the Library of Congress and studied military strategy. During the war, Lincoln helped Northern generals plan many of the battles. Sometimes he went to visit the troops.

The Union had a three-part plan for winning the war. First, Lincoln ordered a **blockade** of the Southern ports. This would keep the Confederacy from traveling

at sea to get supplies or sell its crops. Second, the Union would invade the South and divide it into sections. The last part of the plan was to attack Richmond, Virginia, the new capital of the Confederacy.

At first, the Confederacy won most of the battles. The North did not have any military leaders that compared with the Southern general Robert E. Lee. Lee was an experienced and respected military man, having served in the Mexican War. In fact, Lincoln first asked Robert E. Lee to command the Union army. Although Lee was not in favor of secession, and thought slavery was wrong, he decided he could not fight against the people of his native state of Virginia. With a heavy heart, he resigned from the U.S. Army, writing, "I hope I may never be called upon to draw

Lincoln visited the site where soldiers were fighting the Battle of Antietam in the fall of 1862. President Lincoln took an active role in the war. He helped Union generals plan their battles and visited their troops.

Among the many people who visited President Lincoln at the White House was Sojourner Truth. She was a former slave who fought fiercely against slavery. After her visit, Truth said, "I am proud to say that I never was treated with more kindness and cordiality than I was by the great and good man Abraham Lincoln." At right is a photograph of Sojourner Truth that was combined with a photograph of Lincoln.

Early in the war, Union armies used hot air balloons to see where Confederate troops were. From an altitude of 300 feet (91 m), the balloons allowed Union soldiers to see for more than 15 miles (24 km).

Many of the soldiers who fought in the Civil War were very young. About 100,000 of them were under the age of 16.

my sword." Robert E. Lee went on to become the greatest general of the Civil War.

General George McClellan, the commander of the Union armies, was good at organizing, but he was afraid to use his army in battle. There were some victories in Tennessee for the Union, but many thousands of men on both sides were killed in bloody battles. Union armies could not capture Richmond.

In addition to conducting the war, President Lincoln also spent a lot of time greeting visitors at the White House. Every day people lined up to see him. When his secretaries saw how tired these endless visits left him, they tried to limit the visiting hours, but Lincoln said that he must talk to all who came.

Lincoln used these meetings, along with White House receptions, to find out what people thought of his **policies.** He knew he had to get citizens to support the Union armies. He found that many people were willing to fight to preserve the Union, but they would not fight to end slavery. Others felt that ending slavery should be the highest goal of the Civil War. Knowing how people felt helped Lincoln figure out the best time to announce new policies to the public.

The states between the North and the South, called the border states, had not joined the Confederacy. These included Kentucky, Missouri, Delaware, and Maryland. Although they were part of the Union, the citizens of these states still kept slaves. Lincoln knew that if slavery were suddenly **abolished,** these states would join the Confederacy. This would make it much more difficult for the Union to win the war. President Lincoln declared many times that the purpose of the war was to preserve the Union, not to abolish slavery. This position made **abolitionists** angry, but it kept the border states from seceding.

The Civil War was often called "The Brothers' War" because of the many families divided by loyalties to either the Union or to the Confederacy. One typical story is that of a Confederate soldier who was captured by Union forces—and found that one of his captors was his own brother.

FAMILY LIFE

Lincoln had little time to relax and enjoy his time in the White House. Because of the Civil War, he was busy and worried much of the time. Sometimes he would take a carriage ride with his wife, and he enjoyed going to the theater when he could. Probably his greatest pleasure was playing with his two youngest sons, Willie and Tad. He wrestled with them and took them along when he visited troops near Washington, D.C.

Lincoln wanted his boys to have a lot of freedom, and they were allowed to run wild in the White House. They would slide down banisters, interrupt important meetings, and play tricks on the people who worked there. They dragged their father to see plays they put on in the attic. They held "circuses" with the many animals they kept. Tad even slept with a pet goat on his bed!

In 1850, the Lincolns had lost their second son, Eddie, to illness. He was only three years old, and Mary and Abraham were heartbroken. They had to face yet another terrible loss in 1862, when 11-year-old Willie died of a fever. Lincoln was sadder than he had ever been, and Mary would not go outside for several months. Tad was lonely, trailing around behind his father. Life for the Lincoln family was never the same after Willie's death.

VICTORY AND FREEDOM

The war was going badly for the Union. The army under General McClellan was weak and indecisive. McClellan trained the new recruits with care, but month after month he still failed to move against the rebel forces that were building up in Virginia. In the western states, the army commanders seemed to be following McClellan's example. The commanders said their troops were still being trained and were not ready to fight. Members of Congress and the public were frustrated. They questioned whether Lincoln was a strong enough leader for the Union.

Lincoln was impatient, too, and could see that the war needed a new sense of purpose. Late in 1862, President Lincoln announced the change in his position on slavery. Although he had always thought slavery was wrong, he now saw several reasons to make a stronger statement against it. For one thing, he knew that more people in the North were turning against slavery. He also knew that many European countries thought slavery was a horrible thing. He believed they would be more willing to support the Union if

It is estimated that 180,000 black soldiers served in the Union army during the war. Among these men, 23 earned the Medal of Honor.

they knew it was fighting to end slavery. Also, many slaves were running away from their owners. If they were legally free, they could serve as soldiers in the Union army.

On January 1, 1863, President Lincoln signed the **Emancipation** Proclamation, a document stating that all slaves in the rebelling states were "forever free." "If my name ever goes into history," he said, "it will be for this act."

The Emancipation Proclamation didn't actually free any slaves. For one thing, the Union could not enforce its laws in the Confederate states because they were no longer part of the nation. Also, the Emancipation Proclamation didn't apply to the loyal border states

The Emancipation Proclamation made some people angry. Many Northerners believed it did not do enough to end slavery. Southerners believed that Lincoln had no right to tell them what to do. After all, they no longer considered him their president.

Mary Todd Lincoln had a difficult time during her husband's presidency. Because of the war, she held fewer parties than the first ladies before her, so some people criticized her for not inviting guests into the president's home. Others said she spent too much money on clothing. These insults hurt Mrs. Lincoln at first, but after her son Willie died, she no longer cared. His loss devastated her.

because Lincoln did not want to risk making them angry enough to leave the Union. He repeatedly urged the border states to voluntarily free their slaves. He even promised that the U.S. government would help pay the owners for their losses. But citizens in these states did not take his advice. Lincoln was greatly disappointed. Still, this was the beginning of the end of slavery in the United States. The Emancipation Proclamation gave new purpose to the war. It also laid the groundwork for the 13th **Amendment** to the Constitution, which would end slavery in 1865.

Even though the Emancipation Proclamation didn't actually free them, many slaves ran away from their owners. Thousands of freed slaves later joined the Union

Lincoln had trouble finding a good general until he met Ulysses S. Grant. General Grant won nearly every battle he fought. Early in 1864, Lincoln put him in charge of all the Union armies.

army. Several elite black combat units were formed. The most famous of these was the 54th Massachusetts. This unit was led by socially prominent white officers who believed that slavery was wrong.

In May of 1863, General Ulysses S. Grant's Union forces surrounded Vicksburg, Mississippi. They bombarded the Confederate Army with cannons until it surrendered on July 4. When an army surrenders, it gives up and admits defeat. With this victory, the Union had control of the Mississippi River, separating the states east of the river from those in the West. This was an important victory because it meant that Union troops could now move troops and supplies freely on the river, and they could also prevent Southern troops from doing the same.

In July, the Battle of Gettysburg in Pennsylvania left 60,000 men killed or wounded before General Lee retreated. On November 19, 1863, Lincoln was asked to speak at the dedication of a cemetery at Gettysburg. He spoke for only about three minutes, but that speech, known as the Gettysburg Address, would be remembered all over the world as a statement of the ideals of American democracy.

In March of 1864, Lincoln put Ulysses S. Grant in charge of all the Union armies. Grant commanded the armies near Washington and sent General William T. Sherman to take command in Tennessee. By early summer, Grant had almost surrounded Richmond. The Confederacy was close to collapse. In Tennessee, Sherman marched eastward with 100,000 Union troops and captured Atlanta, Georgia. Then he began his famous March to the Sea. As they marched to Savannah, Georgia, on the Atlantic coast, the Northern army destroyed almost everything in its path. They weakened the South still more as they burned homes, fields, and mills and drove off farm animals.

In the summer of 1864, Lincoln decided to take the final step toward ending slavery. He called for an amendment to the Constitution that would make slavery illegal everywhere in the United States. Lincoln's opponents in the North were outraged. They felt that the war was justified to preserve the Union, but were against freeing the slaves, who could then compete for jobs. Many people, including Lincoln and his advisers, felt certain that he would not be reelected in the fall

While living in the White House, Mary Todd Lincoln's best friend was a former slave named Elizabeth Keckley. She was a well-known dressmaker in Washington D.C. and comforted Mary after Willie Lincoln's death. Elizabeth also told Mary about her life as a slave, causing Mary to become strongly opposed to slavery. The two friends did much to help runaway slaves in Washington D.C. They donated blankets, food, and other necessities.

election. But in spite of the rising criticism, the recent Union victories helped to shore up support for Lincoln. It was becoming clear that the Confederacy could not hold out much longer. The Southern armies were being defeated one after another, and they were not able to replace their dead soldiers. In spite of all the criticism, Lincoln was reelected in November 1864.

By the time Lincoln started his second term early in 1865, the end of the war was in sight. In his second inaugural address, Lincoln urged people to end the war without hatred and to heal the country's wounds. He asked people "to do all which may achieve and cherish a just and lasting peace among ourselves and with all nations."

That spring, Grant captured the railroads that brought supplies into Richmond. On April 9, 1865, General Lee was forced to surrender at Appomattox Courthouse in Virginia. When Grant asked Lincoln what should happen to Lee's men, Lincoln said that he wanted no man punished. He said to let them keep their horses to help plant their spring crops.

The war had been very difficult for President Lincoln, but he had done everything he could to win it. He was deeply saddened by the hundreds of thousands of young men who had died on both sides. He had slept little and eaten poorly. He had rarely found time to relax. And yet, his kind and gentle nature never left him. There are hardly any accounts of Lincoln speaking

This is one of the last photographs taken of President Lincoln. The stress and strain of dealing with four years of war can be seen in his tired face. Though he was only 56 years old, he looked much older.

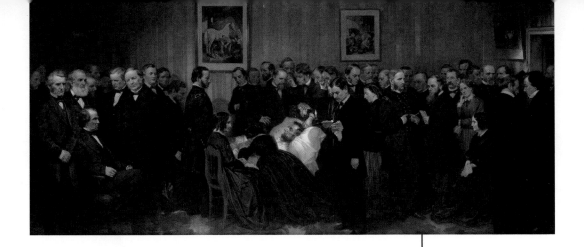

harshly or bitterly to anyone through all the dark years of the war.

President Lincoln was looking forward to the work of rebuilding the nation after the terrible destruction of the war. He and Mary talked about traveling to Europe, Jerusalem, and California after his term was over. Then they hoped to settle down to a quiet life in Springfield. But he would never do any of these things.

Just five days after Lee's surrender, the Lincolns were watching a play at Ford's Theatre in Washington. John Wilkes Booth, a famous actor and bitter anti-Unionist, crept up behind Lincoln and shot him in the head. Lincoln was carried to a room across the street from the theater. He died early the next morning, on April 15, 1865.

Many people think that Abraham Lincoln was America's greatest president. From his rough frontier childhood, he grew up to become a brilliant leader. Even today, his powerful speeches help us to remember Lincoln's faith in the Declaration of Independence—his belief that "all men are created equal." He freed the slaves and kept the country from breaking apart. He proved to the world that democracy could work.

Abraham Lincoln died on April 15, 1865. The people of the United States could no longer rely on his leadership to help restore the tattered nation.

THE DRAFT RIOTS

When President Lincoln first called for volunteers at the beginning of the Civil War, thousands of men enlisted in the Union army. In fact, many had to be turned away because there were not enough guns for them. Later in the war, it was a different story. Thousands of volunteers had been killed in the war. Many people in the North were not willing to fight to free the slaves.

To solve the problem of not having enough soldiers, Lincoln instituted the first **draft** in March of 1863. All men between the ages of 18 and 45 were required to join local army units and be available to fight in the war. There were two exceptions written into the law. Men could avoid joining the army if they hired a substitute to replace them, or if they paid the government $300.00. To many, it seemed unfair that rich people could pay their way out of military service, while poor men did not have the choice. As a result, people formed secret societies to organize against the draft. Violence erupted in several Northern cities. The worst draft riots were in New York City. An anti-draft mob attacked draft officers, soldiers, and policemen. Black people were chased down and killed. Finally, the government called on troops from Gettysburg to restore order. Over 100 people died and more than a million dollars' worth of property was destroyed in New York City during the worst of the draft riots.

THE GETTYSBURG ADDRESS

When the armies buried some 40,000 dead soldiers at Gettysburg, the bodies didn't stay buried. Rain uncovered thousands of them, and the people of Gettysburg knew they had to do something. With the help of Northern governors, they raised money to create the National Soldiers' Cemetery on the battlefield. Then they reburied the dead.

The ceremony to dedicate the cemetery was held on November 19, 1863. Between 15,000 and 20,000 people gathered to take part in the event. The main speaker was Edward Everett, America's leading speechmaker at that time. He spoke for two hours. President Lincoln also spoke at the event. When it was his turn, he rose, put on his glasses, and took two sheets of paper from his pocket. His speech was about three minutes long. When Lincoln returned to his seat, the audience was quiet. Many of the people were disappointed. Some say that Lincoln himself felt the speech had been a failure. Some newspapers reported that it was dull, but others said it was a work of genius.

It was, in fact, an important speech. In simple, beautiful words, Lincoln asked that people remember the ideals for which the soldiers had fought. He asked them to remember the Declaration of Independence, which says that all men are created equal. He said the soldiers who fought for this ideal did not die for nothing, but to preserve democracy. Lincoln reminded his audience that the soldiers gave their lives to prove that "government of the people, by the people, for the people, shall not perish from the earth."

1800	1810	1820	1830	1840

1809
Abraham Lincoln is born on February 12 at Sinking Spring Farm, near what is now Hodgenville, Kentucky. His parents were Thomas Lincoln and Nancy Hanks Lincoln.

1811
Lincoln moves to Knob Creek with his parents and his sister, Sarah. This is the first home he will remember.

1815
Lincoln goes to school for the first time and learns to read and write.

1816
The family moves to Indiana to start a new farm. Lincoln will remember the trip as the hardest experience of his life.

1818
Lincoln's mother dies.

1819
Thomas Lincoln marries Sarah Bush Johnston.

1828
Lincoln takes a flatboat 1,200 miles down the Ohio and Mississippi Rivers to New Orleans.

1830
Lincoln helps his family move to Illinois. He stays to help build the house and start the farm before setting off on his own.

1831
Lincoln takes another boatload of cargo to New Orleans with his cousin and stepbrother. In July, he goes to live in New Salem, Illinois.

1832
Lincoln is elected captain of a volunteer militia.

1833
Lincoln becomes the New Salem postmaster, earning about $50 a year.

1834
Lincoln is elected to the Illinois state legislature for the first time. He goes on to be reelected for three more two-year terms and serves for a total of eight years.

1837
After studying law for nearly three years, Lincoln passes his exams and is admitted into law practice on March 1.

1842
Lincoln marries Mary Todd on November 4.

1843
The Lincolns' first son, Robert Todd, is born.

1844
The Lincolns move to a house in Springfield where they go on to live for the next 17 years. It is the only house that Lincoln ever owns.

1846
The Lincolns' second son, Eddie, is born. Lincoln is elected to the United States House of Representatives. He serves a single two-year term.

1850

Eddie Lincoln dies of an illness at the age of three. The Lincolns' third son, Willie, is born.

1853

The Lincolns' fourth son, Thomas, is born. His parents call him Tad.

1854

Congress passes the Kansas-Nebraska Act, opening the spread of slavery to new territories. Lincoln, who had been losing interest in politics, neglects his law practice and speaks out against the Act.

1856

Lincoln joins the Republican Party, which opposes slavery.

1858

Lincoln wins the Republican nomination for the U.S. Senate and launches his campaign with a fiery speech against the idea of a country that is half slave and half free. In the summer, Lincoln challenges the Democratic candidate, Stephen Douglas, to a series of debates, which make Lincoln well known around the country.

1860

Lincoln is chosen as the Republican candidate for the presidency. He is elected on November 6. In December, South Carolina announces that it is seceding from the Union and is dedicated to the preservation of slavery.

1861

Lincoln takes office on March 4. On April 12, Confederate cannons fire on Fort Sumter, and the Civil War begins. Lincoln immediately calls for 75,000 volunteers to join the Union army. The Battle of Bull Run takes place in July a few miles from Washington, D.C. Union troops under General Irwin McDowell break ranks and flee back to Washington.

1862

Willie Lincoln dies of fever in February, sending Lincoln into a deep depression. Union troops win battles at Fort Henry, Fort Donelson, and Shiloh under General Ulysses S. Grant.

1863

Lincoln signs the Emancipation Proclamation, a document freeing the slaves in the Confederate states. In July, General Grant's armies conquer Vicksburg, Mississippi, gaining control of the Mississippi River. Union armies win the Battle of Gettysburg. In November, Lincoln delivers the Gettysburg Address.

1864

General Grant takes command of all Union armies. In September, General Sherman's troops capture Atlanta. In November, they begin their March to the Sea in Georgia.

1865

On January 31, the House of Representatives introduces the 13th Amendment to officially end slavery in the United States. Lincoln takes the oath of office on March 4 to begin his second term as president. On April 9, Confederate General Robert E. Lee surrenders at Appomattox Courthouse in Virginia. Lincoln is shot by John Wilkes Booth at Ford's Theatre on April 14. He dies the next morning. On December 18, 1865, eight months after Lincoln's death, the 13th Amendment is approved.

GLOSSARY

abolished (uh-BALL-isht) If something is abolished, it has been stopped or ended. The Southern states did not want to abolish slavery.

abolitionists (ab-uh-LISH-uh-nists) Abolitionists were people who wanted to put an end to slavery before and during the Civil War. Abolitionists wanted President Lincoln to end slavery in all the states.

amendment (uh-MEND-ment) An amendment is a change or addition to the Constitution or other document. The 13th Amendment outlawed slavery in the United States.

blockade (blah-KAYD) A blockade keeps people and supplies from moving in or out of an area. A blockade of the Southern ports caused the people of the South to lose money because they couldn't sell their crops to European markets.

campaign (kam-PAYN) A campaign is the process of running for an election, including activities such as giving speeches or attending rallies. Lincoln's campaign in 1860 was successful, and he was elected president.

cases (KAY-sez) Cases are matters decided by a court of law. Lawyers argue cases in court before a judge.

Confederate (kun-FED-uh-ret) A Confederate was a person who lived in, supported, or fought for the Confederate States of America during the Civil War. The Confederates seceded from the Union.

constitution (kon-stuh-TOO-shun) A constitution is the set of basic principles that govern a state, country, or society. The Confederates wrote their own constitution.

convention (kun-VEN-shun) A convention is a meeting. Abraham Lincoln was nominated for president at the Republican National Convention in 1860.

debating (dih-BAY-ting) Debating means taking part in a contest in which opponents argue for opposite sides of an issue. Lincoln was good at debating.

documents (DOK-yuh-ments) Documents are written or printed papers that give people important information. The Emancipation Proclamation was a document written to free slaves in the South.

draft (DRAFT) A system of choosing a person or persons for service in the armed forces. During the Civil War, most young men were drafted, required to be available to join the Union army.

emancipation (ee-man-seh-PAY-shun) Emancipation is the act of setting someone free. The Emancipation Proclamation set slaves free in the rebelling states.

ferry (FAYR-ee) A ferry is a boat used to transport people and goods. A ferry took the Lincolns, their two horses, and all their belongings across the Ohio River.

frontier (frun-TEER) A frontier is a region that is at the edge of or beyond settled land. In Lincoln's youth, Kentucky was part of the U.S. frontier.

inaugural address (ih-NAWG-yuh-rul uh-DRESS) An inaugural address is the speech that an elected president makes at his inauguration. An inauguration is the ceremony that takes place when a new president begins a term.

latitude (LAT-uh-tood) Latitude is the distance of a place as measured north or south from the equator. On globes and maps, lines of latitude run east and west. The latitude of the southern border of Missouri marked the point south of which slavery was legal.

nominated (NOM-uh-nay-tid) If a political party nominated someone, it chose him or her to run for a political office. Each party holds a convention to nominate a presidential candidate.

plantations (plan-TAY-shunz) Plantations are large farms or groups of farms that grow crops such as tobacco, sugarcane, or cotton. Southern plantations depended on the labor of slaves to grow their crops.

policies (PAWL-uh-seez) Policies are rules made to help run a government or other organization. Lincoln wanted to know what people thought of his policies.

political parties (puh-LIT-uh-kul PAR-teez) Political parties are groups of people who share similar ideas about how to run a government. Lincoln joined the Republican Party in 1856.

politician (pawl-uh-TISH-un) Politicians are people who run for elected offices. As a child, Lincoln imitated politicians giving speeches.

politics (PAWL-uh-tiks) Politics refers to the actions and practices of the government. Lincoln returned to politics because he did not want slavery to spread.

precinct (PREE-sinkt) A precinct is a district of a city or a town. Most of the people in Lincoln's precinct voted for him when he ran for Illinois state legislature in 1832.

preserve (preh-ZERV) If people preserve something, they keep it from harm or change. Lincoln wanted to preserve the Union.

provisions (pro-VIZH-unz) Provisions are a stock of necessary items, especially food. The soldiers at Fort Sumter were running out of provisions before the Civil War began.

Republican Party (ree-PUB-lih-ken PAR-tee) The Republican Party is one of the two major U.S. political parties. President Lincoln was a Republican.

seceded (suh-SEE-ded) If a group seceded, it separated from a larger group. South Carolina was the first state to secede from the Union.

session (SESH-un) A session is a series of meetings of a legislative body. When Lincoln was in office the yearly session for the Illinois state legislature lasted about 100 days.

state legislature (STAYT LEJ-uh-slay-chur) A state legislature is the part of a state's government that makes laws. Lincoln was elected to the Illinois state legislature four times in a row.

supreme court (suh-PREEM KORT) A supreme court is usually the most powerful court in an individual state. Lincoln took cases to the Illinois Supreme Court when he worked as a lawyer.

terms (TERMZ) Terms are the length of time politicians can keep their positions by law. In Lincoln's time, a term in the lower house of the Illinois state legislature was two years.

territories (TAYR-ih-tor-eez) Territories are lands or regions, especially lands that belong to a government. The Kansas-Nebraska Act said that all new territories should decide for themselves if they wanted slavery to be legal.

Union (YOON-yen) The Union is another name for the United States of America. During the Civil War, the North was called the Union.

widow (WID-oh) A widow is a woman whose husband has died. Lincoln's father married a widow named Sarah Bush Johnston.

THE UNITED STATES GOVERNMENT

The United States government is divided into three equal branches: the executive, the legislative, and the judicial. This division helps prevent abuses of power because each branch has to answer to the other two. No one branch can become too powerful.

EXECUTIVE BRANCH

PRESIDENT
VICE PRESIDENT
DEPARTMENTS

The job of the executive branch is to enforce the laws. It is headed by the president, who serves as the spokesperson for the United States around the world. The president signs bills into law and appoints important officials such as federal judges. He or she is also the commander in chief of the U.S. military. The president is assisted by the vice president, who takes over if the president dies or cannot carry out the duties of the office.

The executive branch also includes various departments, each focused on a specific topic. They include the Defense Department, the Justice Department, and the Agriculture Department. The department heads, along with other officials such as the vice president, serve as the president's closest advisers, called the cabinet.

LEGISLATIVE BRANCH

CONGRESS
Senate and
House of Representatives

The job of the legislative branch is to make the laws. It consists of Congress, which is divided into two parts: the Senate and the House of Representatives. The Senate has 100 members, and the House of Representatives has 435 members. Each state has two senators. The number of representatives a state has varies depending on the state's population.

Besides making laws, Congress also passes budgets and enacts taxes. In addition, it is responsible for declaring war, maintaining the military, and regulating trade with other countries.

JUDICIAL BRANCH

SUPREME COURT
COURTS OF APPEALS
DISTRICT COURTS

The job of the judicial branch is to interpret the laws. It consists of the nation's federal courts. Trials are held in district courts. During trials, judges must decide what laws mean and how they apply. Courts of appeals review the decisions made in district courts.

The nation's highest court is the Supreme Court. If someone disagrees with a court of appeals ruling, he or she can ask the Supreme Court to review it. The Supreme Court may refuse. The Supreme Court makes sure that decisions and laws do not violate the Constitution.

CHOOSING
THE PRESIDENT

I t may seem odd, but American voters don't elect the president directly. Instead, the president is chosen using what is called the Electoral College.

Each state gets as many votes in the Electoral College as its combined total of senators and representatives in Congress. For example, Iowa has two senators and five representatives, so it gets seven electoral votes. Although the District of Columbia does not have any voting members in Congress, it gets three electoral votes. Usually, the candidate who wins the most votes in any given state receives all of that state's electoral votes.

To become president, a candidate must get more than half of the Electoral College votes. There are a total of 538 votes in the Electoral College, so a candidate needs 270 votes to win. If nobody receives 270 Electoral College votes, the House of Representatives chooses the president.

With the Electoral College system, the person who receives the most votes nationwide does not always receive the most electoral votes. This happened most recently in 2000, when Al Gore received half a million more national votes than George W. Bush. Bush became president because he had more Electoral College votes.

THE WHITE HOUSE

The White House is the official home of the president of the United States. It is located at 1600 Pennsylvania Avenue NW in Washington, D.C. In 1792, a contest was held to select the architect who would design the president's home. James Hoban won. Construction took eight years.

The first president, George Washington, never lived in the White House. The second president, John Adams, moved into the house in 1800, though the inside was not yet complete. During the War of 1812, British soldiers burned down much of the White House. It was rebuilt several years later.

The White House was changed through the years. Porches were added, and President Theodore Roosevelt added the West Wing. President William Taft changed the shape of the presidential office, making it into the famous Oval Office. While Harry Truman was president, the old house was discovered to be structurally weak. All the walls were reinforced with steel, and the rooms were rebuilt.

Today, the White House has 132 rooms (including 35 bathrooms), 28 fireplaces, and 3 elevators. It takes 570 gallons of paint to cover the outside of the six-story building. The White House provides the president with many ways to relax. It includes a putting green, a jogging track, a swimming pool, a tennis court, and beautifully landscaped gardens. The White House also has a movie theater, a billiard room, and a one-lane bowling alley.

PRESIDENTIAL PERKS

The job of president of the United States is challenging. It is probably one of the most stressful jobs in the world. Because of this, presidents are paid well, though not nearly as well as the leaders of large corporations. In 2007, the president earned $400,000 a year. Presidents also receive extra benefits that make the demanding job a little more appealing.

★ **Camp David:** In the 1940s, President Franklin D. Roosevelt chose this heavily wooded spot in the mountains of Maryland to be the presidential retreat, where presidents can relax. Even though it is a retreat, world business is conducted there. Most famously, President Jimmy Carter met with Middle Eastern leaders at Camp David in 1978. The result was a peace agreement between Israel and Egypt.

★ *Air Force One:* The president flies on a jet called *Air Force One*. It is a Boeing 747-200B that has been modified to meet the president's needs.

Air Force One is the size of a large home. It is equipped with a dining room, sleeping quarters, a conference room, and office space. It also has two kitchens that can provide food for up to 50 people.

★ **The Secret Service:** While not the most glamorous of the president's perks, the Secret Service is one of the most important. The Secret Service is a group of highly trained agents who protect the president and the president's family.

★ **The Presidential State Car:** The presidential limousine is a stretch Cadillac DTS.

It has been armored to protect the president in case of attack. Inside the plush car are a foldaway desk, an entertainment center, and a communications console.

★ **The Food:** The White House has five chefs who will make any food the president wants. The White House also has an extensive wine collection.

★ **Retirement:** A former president receives a pension, or retirement pay, of just under $180,000 a year. Former presidents also receive Secret Service protection for the rest of their lives.

FACTS

QUALIFICATIONS

To run for president, a candidate must

* ★ be at least 35 years old
* ★ be a citizen who was born in the United States
* ★ have lived in the United States for 14 years

TERM OF OFFICE

A president's term of office is four years.
No president can stay in office for more than two terms.

ELECTION DATE

The presidential election takes place every four years on the first Tuesday of November.

INAUGURATION DATE

Presidents are inaugurated on January 20.

OATH OF OFFICE

I do solemnly swear I will faithfully execute the office of the President of the United States and will to the best of my ability preserve, protect, and defend the Constitution of the United States.

WRITE A LETTER TO THE PRESIDENT

One of the best things about being a U.S. citizen is that Americans get to participate in their government. They can speak out if they feel government leaders aren't doing their jobs. They can also praise leaders who are going the extra mile. Do you have something you'd like the president to do? Should the president worry more about the environment and encourage people to recycle? Should the government spend more money on our schools? You can write a letter to the president to say how you feel!

1600 Pennsylvania Avenue
Washington, D.C. 20500
You can even send an e-mail to: president@whitehouse.gov

BOOKS

Collard, Sneed B. *Abraham Lincoln: A Courageous Leader.*
New York: Benchmark Books, 2006.

Collier, James Lincoln. *The Abraham Lincoln You
Never Knew.* Children's Press, 2004.

Herbert, Janis. *Abraham Lincoln For Kids: His Life and Times
With 21 Activities.* Chicago: Chicago Review Press, 2007.

Mattern, Joanne. *The Big Book of the Civil War; Fascinating
Facts About the Civil War, Including Historical Photographs,
Maps and Documents.* Courage Books, 2007.

Pinkney, Andrea Davis. *Abraham Lincoln: Letters From A
Slave Girl (Dear Mr. President).* Winslow Press, 2001.

Stone, Tanya Lee. *Abraham Lincoln.* New York: DK
Children, 2005.

VIDEOS

Abraham Lincoln: Preserving the Union. DVD (New York:
A & E Home Video, 2004).

*American Experience: Abraham and Mary Lincoln: A House
Divided.* DVD (Alexandria, VA: PBS Home Video, 2005).

The American President. DVD, VHS (Alexandria, VA: PBS
Home Video, 2000).

The History Channel Presents The Presidents. DVD (New
York: A & E Home Video, 2005).

National Geographic's Inside the White House. DVD
(Washington, D.C.: National Geographic Video, 2003).

INTERNET SITES

Visit our Web page for lots of links about
Abraham Lincoln and other U.S. presidents:

http://www.childsworld.com/links

Note to Parents, Teachers, and Librarians: We routinely verify our Web links to make
sure they are safe, active sites—so encourage your readers to check them out!

INDEX